T0304484

"What does it mean to be 'proving poetry to one another'? What to find skin you recognize, skin that smells of citrus? Lourdes Figueroa is a poem weaver of the highest order. These words pant and breathe. These poems are some birds, some kisses, some city buses. These poems are the product of a muscular and questing curiosity. Enter and be changed."

KIM SHUCK
7th Poet Laureate of San Francisco

"*Vuelta* writes itself like 'a series / of sprints.' The poem unfolds, turning and returning to itself in its many mergings of languages, sounds, scents, feels and images. In the Nahuatl language, a poem is *in xóchitl in chicatl*, 'flower' and 'song,' a *difrasismo*, a binary. Lourdes Figueroa claims *Nepantla*, the blending, mixing, threshold—past, present and future—'a song we sang together,' a song you inhabit, the freeing up of the heart, the people, the pueblo through the language of syncretism, and exuberance, a becoming, a dreaming, 'sand on some beach.' The poet is a proud *marimacha*, queer, a baby dyke, gay, *joteando, a lover, pocha, chicana, Lesbiana*, 'the whole / body of america.' They tell of 'love moving from landscape to landscape,' of the *colibri and the quetzal*, the *cempaxuchitl* and *hatzav* flowers, of Juan Diego's 'impossible roses,' of La Llorona, the weeping woman, and rituals like the day of the dead and the mown grass of a soccer field, el *azádon* in Idaho, the smell of an old·leather baseball glove and the *revoltijos / de amor*. The poet sings '*america / I am reclaiming you in verb*' and does just that. –Norma Cole, author of Fate News"

NORMA COLE
author of *Fate News*

"This collection will break you apart in a soft palm, scatter you on the breeze slipping across damp skin, return you to yourself with a shuddering breath. Here is the body, each clamorous cell humming and hungry. Here are words that wail and whisper, that caress, that ring a challenge off every sharp edge. Here is the promise/audacity of petals opening, a broken heart beating, wings taking flight. Above all, here is love."

J. WORTHEN

"Lourdes Figueroa's *Vuelta* is full of incandescent writing that burns the vapor off words, leaving only what is essential behind. Here we read of queer love and desire, of coming of age, and of migration, both as a global phenomenon demonstrated by the figure of the monarch butterfly and as the far more personal, localized story of a Mexican girl in Idaho re/claiming American identity through, among other things, a fascination with baseball. Language, too, becomes part of the story, in the sense of both bilingual existence and the power of saying to break the fourth wall. As Figueroa writes, 'but we all did it / as we proved / poetry to each other / the verb collapsing / into nothing / & everything / shining / like a mirage.'"

JENNY DRAI
author of *The History Worker*

"Reading *Vuelta* is playing baseball in fields where wilderness is beneath every step and intertwined in each breath. In the planting, in the harvest and the cityscapes far beyond love is made, false selves undone, reunification occurs with the forgotten angels. "

MONICA ZARAZUA
author of *Slide*

"This is an impressive and breathtaking gathering of poems. The work left me feeling powerful, inspired and a little salty and sweaty, which is one of my favorite ways to be! The imagery left blossoms of envy all over my mouth, green flowers for how jealous I am of Lourdes Figueroa's talent as a writer. Every part of the worlds that Figueroa creates in this book is a poem, from the ground, to the seagulls, to a locker room, to the weight of lust and beauty she fiercely crafts into a very moving experience. This book has a heart beat, Lourdes Figueroa shows you that, then surprises you with the humor. Figureroa's book made me cry one moment, and then leap up off my couch screaming 'to grab my nalgas ,means your truth!' YES! Which is one of my many favorite lines in the book. Part call to action, part power love song to a todas las marimachas, you gotta read this book! –Baruch Porras-Hernandez, Host & head organizer of¿Donde esta mi gente? author of the chapbooks 'I Miss You, Delicate' and 'Lovers of the Deep Fried Circle' with Sibling Rivalry Press"

BARUCH PORRAS-HERNANDEZ
host & head organizer of *¿Donde esta mi gente?*
author of *I Miss You, Delicate* and
Lovers of the Deep Fried Circle

"In *Vuelta*, Lourdes Figueroa unfurls the sensuality of revolt, of what it means to turn and return to love as a devout prayer/poem/an intimate saunter into a new city. Here, the flowers bloom, and 'the long poem is nothing but the weeping of a prayer.' The body is not a body, but the topography of memory for exploration between lovers. Spanish and English bind around Americana roots as the testament of where survival becomes transcendence, of where 'la cicatriz es nuestra lengua'/the scar is our tongue. *Vuelta* is an incredible amorous force unabashedly stamped–– by 'ESA LESBIANA.' Pouring sensuality into a steaming pot of boiling floral petals, Lourdes Figueroa is *that* new/queer/Latinx/Chingona/ poet to be reckoned with, to have us all walk away with 'how love walks on two feet.'"

THEA MATTHEWS
author of *Unearth [The Flowers]*

"What does it mean to write about Love at the end of the world? What honeyed worlds of resilience emerge *at the cusp of wind & spit* where memoria y sueños are most tender and human? Figueroa dreams vivid Brown visions reclaiming Americana and illuminating a Queer futurity of fierce softness, salted desire, and cosmically tender Love. Vuelta is a vital and volant hymnal of migrating generational energies *surviving making el mundo dar vueltas* - this collection asks its reader to become a colibri and remember '*the dream is always/ bursting / into something else.*' "

ANGEL DOMINGUEZ
author of *Desgraciado (the collected letters)*

"Lourdes Figueroa's *Vuelta* inhales the ecstatic and exhales the erotic. In these poems where 'the dream is always/ bursting/ into something else,' words burst into breath, and wonder into lust. There's a headiness in these poems' music and dreamscapes, yet readers are always called back by the full flesh and love 'stink' of the body: '*aquí besitos on your cutis*'. Figueroa is a poet of duendes, of secrets hidden in mixed tongues, of many returns. These poems remind us of our transience & transcendence, of homes where 'we found ourselves/ at the cusp of wind & spit/ the awning of our ribcage/ shaped like a media naranja...'"

KAREN LLAGAS
author of *All Of Us Are Cleaved & Archipelago Dust*

"Una poeta profeta that speaks through a yellow mirror upon which antepasados en forma de marisposas alight and whose voice gives the land's own erotic desire her shape. Memory throbs as brown nipple, as tongue aching for the salt of a lover's neck; blossoms as cempax-uchíl. In your hands, these poems bleed the acute longing fragrance of almendra, with the knowing grit of that very Bay Area gesture of passing the joint back and forth silently with your lover. What can I say? These are some sexy, sexy poems."

TATIANA LUBOVISKI-ACOSTA,
author of *La Movida*

"Lourdes Figueroa takes us on a vuelta into the slippery dreamspace of the female body—a place of desire and sanctuary. Yet she does not turn us away from visceral struggle. Let her guide you through this vuelta of skin and sangre, flowers and colibrís, palabras in the mouth and the silences between them, as you enter into ancestral wisdom that flows from one body to another. *Vuelta* will take you out of your body and deep inside it at the same time."

TEHMINA KHAN
poet & professor

"While rooted in the poet's vivid experiences of places such as Yolo county (where she grew up in a family of farmworkers) and San Francisco, *Vuelta* also embodies a transcendent mythopoetic force and prophetic multilingual voice. Set against the backdrop of the world's blade, its colonial violence against migrants, against women, against the earth itself, here's a fierce, cosmic centering of love, particularly of queer, brown love, of revolutionary luminous beauty and erotic power. The Spanish expression dar a luz comes to mind: there's an incantatory momentum, an orality to Figueroa's lines which demand to be read aloud, unfolding in real time unlike ambered, chiseled constructions, rendering the impression of a world birthed anew."

FLORENCIA MILITO
author of *Ituzaingó: Exiles & Reveries*
exilios y ensueños

NOMADIC PRESS

OAKLAND

PHILADELPHIA

XALAPA

WWW.NOMADICPRESS.ORG

MASTHEAD

FOUNDING PUBLISHER
J. K. Fowler

LEAD EDITOR
MK Chavez

ASSOCIATE EDITOR
Michaela Mullin

DESIGN
Jevohn Tyler Newsome

MISSON STATEMENT Through publications, events, and active community participation, Nomadic Press collectively weaves together platforms for intentionally marginalized voices to take their rightful place within the world of the written and spoken word. Through our limited means, we are simply attempting to help right the centuries' old violence and silencing that should never have occurred in the first place and build alliances and community partnerships with others who share a collective vision for a future far better than today.

INVITATIONS Nomadic Press wholeheartedly accepts invitations to read your work during our open reading period every year. To learn more or to extend an invitation, please visit: www.nomadicpress.org/invitations

DISTRIBUTION
Orders by teachers, libraries, trade bookstores, or wholesalers:

Nomadic Press Distribution
orders@nomadicpress.org
(510) 500-5162

Small Press Distribution
spd@spdbooks.org
(510) 524-1668 / (800) 869-7553

This book was made possible by a loving community of chosen family and friends, old and new. For author questions or to book a reading at your bookstore, university/school, or alternative establishment, please send an email to info@nomadicpress.org.

Cover art and author portrait by Arthur Johnstone

Published by Nomadic Press, 1941 Jackson Street, Suite 20, Oakland, CA 94612
First printing, 2023

Library of Congress Cataloging-in-Publication Data

Title: *Vuelta*
p. cm.
Summary: *Vuelta* is a long poem on a quest to recover the body through myth & memory, a reckoning with colonization & the return to our Pachamama. *Vuelta* to revolt, to return, to return, to revoltijo, to revolución, to transform. It is a journey of tongue & breath that asks What's life through the mouth of the queer brown cuerpo. *Vuelta* insists that our bodies are a walking love language miraculously unearthing the beginning & the collapse of time where we allow ourselves to begin again in the same way the monarch continues her journey evolving over & over again.

[1. **POETRY** / LGBTQ+. 2. **POETRY** / American / Latinx. 3. **POETRY** / Subjects & Themes / Nature. 4. **POETRY** / American / General.]

LIBRARY OF CONGRESS CONTROL NUMBER: 2022947170
ISBN: 978-1-955239-40-0

VUELTA

VUELTA

LOURDES FIGUEROA

**NOMADIC
PRESS**

Oakland · Philadelphia · Xalapa

Dame las vueltas de tu corazón/ las voy a poner
en la plaza del pueblo para que sepamos
que el cuerpo es el pueblo/ aquí la hora de amar

CONTENTS

introduction

reading guide

INTRODUCTION

"My first language is breath"—Maria Melendez

I was born within the movements of migration. In my early childhood, I migrated with my parents, up and down from Guadalajara, Mexico to California, United States as they worked in the tomato fields as farm workers. They did this out of necessity. My apá was trying to pay for his studies in medical school. At first, my apá would come with his siblings and his mother to work, but when my amá became pregnant he brought her with him so she could give birth in the United States. They wanted more opportunities for their child.

In the beginning, they always crossed over legally. My apá had his green card, his brother married an American citizen, paid her well; and he requested the rest of the family, my apá, my abuelita, my aunts and uncles. They worked in el azadón because that was what they knew. My abuelito had crossed over during the late 50s as a bracero (this was a program that existed as an agreement between the US and Mexico, as an exchange for cheap labor in agriculture). Abuelito passed on while working in the fields and his death forced my abuelita to work in the States to feed her children. Every year they would make their way to Yuba City, California to work. I was born in Yuba City. Two years later my sister was born there too. In this back and forth, I learned to speak.

It is important that I begin my introduction this way because it was the formation of my language that has brought me to the formation of my poetics, and the formation of this manuscript. It is important to understand that the curves of migration developed and influenced the word that spills from my mouth. It was and is a movement of the earth, following harvest upon harvest. This migration mixed with my mother's song formed my perception of the world in fragments. I write this way, the gut first informing the sound of the poem, then the word written. It is a language of the in-betweens that persists in the work that is constant in my voice. It is the in-betweens of Spanish and English, of gender orientation, sexual orientation, and cultural orientation that breathes the words forward or backward. Autobiographical in its nature.

My first memories of English are silent.

I was enrolled in first grade in Idaho when my parents immigrated to the United States. There I remember the classroom and the playground in silence. I remember focusing hard on the movements of the lips and falling asleep and waking up again to my teacher moving back and forth in front of the chalkboard. After school, my sister and I would listen to the sounds of the television and mimic the sound of English into our Spanish. We would do this throughout our play with our cousins. When I think of that time, I remember the sounds in Spanish, the sounds at home after school. My amá would read to us almost every night. My apá would play us music. We learned our vowels in song, a e i o u, "hay viene la u detrás la o," each letter a dance. With our cousins our play consisted of song, "jugaremos en el bosque mientras el lobo no esta." When the weekends would come, we would either accompany our parents to the fields or if it was payday and their weekend off the entire family would get together, light a fire, eat, drink, sing, and dance cumbias. When they sang, they would close their eyes, letting out the loudest most heartfelt sounds. When they danced, they would move their bodies, close their eyes, and laugh fully moving to the music. Everything seemed to come from their gut.

I am a descendant of song and breath. All of us are. In Mexico there is a day called El día del grito, the day of the scream, the ultimate utterance of scream. It is a painful scream, full of past and present. El día del grito happens on the eve of Mexican Independence Day. Growing up my amá made sure we understood El día del grito. She would make sure that we opened the windows in the evening before midnight and screamed our lungs out until our throats hurt. She would say "andenles abran las ventanas." I would watch her first. She would close her eyes and let out a scream that wasn't coming from her throat but from somewhere else that I couldn't see, her chest, and her stomach contracting tight, and the veins in her throat popping out. There was pain in her face that I could never name when she did this.

In every poem throughout I am slipping into a long tradition that is before me, that is before all of us. Though I sing from the in-betweens, I am slipping into song. The poem existed in oral form before it was written. Sappho's song was passed down orally, generations upon generations before it was formed into written word. In present time it is given to us in fragments, so beautiful. Her song in fragments is what we know and don't know. What don't know is what we feel of her song, where we feel the most intimate of the fragment's movement. The poem is song. I've come to understand this thus far embracing every part of this as much as I can, embracing every imperfection in my voice. Garcia Lorca talks about the deep song, el cante jondo, a song that comes from the deepest cave of the human heart. The gypsy singing in caves, hiding from persecution but singing their word not written, but sung, a pain that can't be explained, it is that part of the fragment that we have. Its full emotion, revolution, its **vuelta**, its full pain is what we don't have before our eyes, that tugs at us and somehow, connects all of us.

I believe in the community of the word. It is to share in lung, voice, and throat. Everyone is a walking poem. Thus, the language that emerges, that is born within my poems, is a language in limbo, not from here or there. It has its own accent and its own rhythm. Its flesh is made of what I speak, and live. Its heart and blood are from the community where I grew up. It is of the people, los chamacos, las chamacas, my neighbors, my amá, my apá, my abuelitas, from friends that I have found, that have found me, and it is from books I continue to encounter in Spanish, Nahualt memory and English. It has its layers that I have yet to uncover that reach even deeper than the Pre-Colombian word.

Each language has its story, its hxstory; and its birth comes from the most intimate that we live and share. Language is an exchange of air, from the throat, from the lungs, from the heart. When born we let out our first word. One can say that it is only a cry. In reality it is a sound coming from within. It is our first exchange with the outside world. Our first communication with what's happening within oneself. It can be pain, fright, I don't know. I don't remember what one feels at birth, but I imagine it's painful, that one feels un chingo de frio. But you see at birth we let out a scream, and this first scream is the most tender, most natural, the most carnal, and the freest of our voice. At this moment our first sound is born, the purest that it can be. I say pure because it is one's actual voice. It's a cry full of oneself, full of everything that we feel emerging towards the exterior, and this air is not mixed with any other form of word, only with what is from within oneself.

I say all of this because each one of us has a sound, we have word, we have song, we have voice, and we have lungs, heart, throat, tongue, and language. With language we get to embrace, listen, cry, hurt each other, smile, and share. All my words are a walking exploration of this. Its direction is clear within each poem and each moment that we manage to share en voz...

VUELTA

Psst...
te quiero contar algo
las estrellas y la luna
me dicen
sobre tu regreso a casa
el viento va pasando
con sus risas
haciéndole cosquillas
a las flores recién nacidas
mientras a cherubim's smile
cackles:

> *según las flowers y su manitas se comen vivas*
> *hundiéndose en sí mismas*
> *preciosa roja morada rosa verdosa*
> *toditas un rainbow bc flowers in general*
> *represent the fragility of life*

*

I slept I dreamt
I woke
& walked to you
there was no/one
dream of you
only the scuffle
of a Colibri's feet

is that possible?

I crave you
seek your breast
above the sun/rise
of your inner thighs I smell
dear beloved
I found my self

encased

within the remnants of a birth
& the roots of an aster flower
she glistened
with the rays of our breath

breasts rising

como la marea
slipping
& we were none
of these things
just wine & verb
verb & rain
rain &
wet skin
eating
color madness

color sadness
color joy
color retorno
all these things
like the budding head
of a purple fig
or fig leaf

we were both inside the memory
of a language dreaming dreams
that look like a mother hawk
flying with her two newborn

                              wing by wing
the seedlings of wheat dancing
letting us know truth
we drunk on revolution
eating & spitting each other
more so crawling & dancing
over bodies
we on top of each
other   *wound*
                              recognizing
                              wound

anointing ourselves
like Jesus's slit gash
the laceration
that led to the other side
torso tongue   *unspeakable cruelties*
vagina bleeding

                    but what is the other side?

we lost the poet
to the scuffle   *un separable love pieces*
of the hummingbird
on the tender branch
of a bamboo tree

                                  is that possible?
                                  to lose a poet?

we couldn't even
see their tiny little feet
but we all did it
as we proved
poetry to each other

                                  pressing her to the muscle of our utero

the verb collapsing
into nothing
& everything
shining
like a mirage
ripple
by ripple
we were both
drinking   *color prophecy our lips growing heavy*
how amazing
this whistle
our earth   *re/turning*

4

& who will dry our eyes?
as we all fall apart

the stars became
flesh
& flesh became
light
& light became
star again
until each of our chest bones
moved like the wings
of a moth flying
& landing on
your bedroom wall
on that corner
of the doorway
where you can
see her whole
wingspan trying to break
a fourth wall with kisses

en esos días comíamos dios

as you lay in bed
with remnants of last night's sleep
tu labios whispering

en mis islas dicen que
la mariposa nocturna
viene del otro lado
un antepasado buscándote
¿será tu abuelita chona?
ella anda aquí mírala

her small body

wide & long
as the eye vision
of hawk as small
as two supple brown
nipples
of corn & wheat
all goldening
as the sun reddens

y los espíritus de anoche
were wearing our botas
the tacón ricocheting
just like the nerve
pulsing on your neck

truth is as I watched you
speak to the moth
I wanted to slip my tongue
on your neck kiss your eyelids
as you went back to sleep
& so I did like everything else
that is meant to be
a love poem about sand
& footprints disappearing
on some beach
it was you
                    all of you
that belonged
in me & I belonged in you
like that abandoned hotel
we thought was haunted

here in California on Hwy 1
maybe it was near Big Sur
I don't remember
much these days
my mind disappears
two baby gays
no, we are two baby dykes
taking a selfie
we belong together
that way
where we both know
the surf will be good
& coffee in the morning
thick & steaming
against the morning breath
against grape vineyards
purple
fog
purple grapes
& fog

*

what scares me the most
is you it has been about 500 years
la cicatriz es nuestra
lengua así como
una vagina morada dando luz
rompiéndose entera

you keep revolving
around the sun
I am nothing

los días enteros
as if no time had passed

I smoke a joint
& pass out
& still the fig tree
blooms
& still

nothing never

we are
digging graves
the earth soft
the earth wet
new buildings
around each other's
abuelitas' ashes

& I can't repeat another poet's metaphor
when their metaphor is a prophecy

& the glint
in a mirror
a mirror
that is flor de cempaxúchitl
color yellow
& a broken heart
all at once

what is it? what is it that you want?
that we want?

isn't the glistening
gold of the wheat
at magic hour meant to be?
& the placenta
after each one of us
thick purple
& meaningful?
carne

carne somos

9

*

I've been hearing
rumors about you
under a swollen moon
                    iluminada por tu recuerdo
could these chismes be true?
about the melancholic angel
we both ran into collecting flowers
that bloom upon summer's departure
& autumn's arrival by a small town's creek
the kind of town that has one stop light
one main street & the smell of mowed alfalfa
                    like a memory coming back to life
we took the angel home
& we slept with their body
licking their sweat bubbles
off their humid pinions
off their nose
off their back
off their middle
between their breasts
we both licked   *agüita de dolor*
& sucked their nipples
their nipples perky
brown & supple
& they felt good on our tongues
our sucking sugared lips
                    upwards
toward the light
of a moon or a star
that is un sol

somewhere further
than Jupiter
as near as mercurio
our tongues salted
& sweetened
with each other's
flesh

> *our wet flesh*
> *our wet womxn*
> *flesh*

*

the echo between our apartment buildings
was the echo of a human chest
la Llorona drunk on the chirp
of a hummingbird & the wetness
of a hatzav flower
a flower that blooms
at the end of Jerusalem's summer
a flower that is impossible here
like the impossible roses
Juan Diego gathered
up in the mount of Tepeyac

¡O Tonantzin!

I lift my eyes
to the wisp of clouds
can you tell
how alike we are?
how honey
drips in the same
amount of time
as your time
can you feel
how tenderly fragile
flowers' petals are

precious burnt honey
papelitos de regalo
deeply soft & thin
what were we
trying to shout?

¿a qué pertenecemos?
if not warmth of bosom
if not my face on your the curve of your clavicle

& between your legs
my face felt so warm
you felt so wet & true
& the song of la Llorona bounced
                    subiendo y bajando con la marea
my curves bounced your skin bounced
we were whole bodies of a tribe of roses
asters hatzavs & marigolds
all of us
all of you
all of me

here's the quetzal
buscándose entre este poema
looking for a peep hole
into the uni/verse
todo un revoltijo
de un quetzal

aquí con otro quetzal
el tiempo húmedo salado
y hermoso

>   *en un mundo*
>   *hay sol mar y*
>   *tierra*

en un mundo
hay carne
y revoltijos
de amor   *agüita de dolor*

somos cadera

>   *pueblitos*

somos sudor

>   *pájaritos*

somos muslo

>   *lágrimas*

somos
los poemas   *marimachitas*
>   *reflejos caminando*
>   *un separable love piece*s

de alguna diosxx
los pedazos de carne
qué más quiere esconder
de las otras diosxxs
somos sus poemas
más íntimos
los más buenos

>   *los que nacen*
>   *en lo hondo*
>   *de su sexo*
>   *húmedo*

*

we found ourselves
at the cusp of wind & spit
the awning of our ribcage
shaped like a media naranja

I am your
media naranja

the mango tree sashays
in the background

you smell of citrus
you smell of oily citrus
& overripe mangoes
the same mangoes
that had fallen tender bruised
yesterday afternoon
today their flesh burst
the brown of your skin
more luminescent

we squinting our eyes
seeing a quetzal tiptoe across
the landscape of our vision
the breeze outside our apartment window
pleasant like the sudden puff
of alas taking flight
cooling our limbs
the angel we both slept with
lingering above us

perching themselves like un sueño
like two dykes like love

cuddling on a sunny Sunday
San Francisco afternoon
the quetzal tethering
herself to la tierra around her
she becoming he all at once
with her golden-green wings
her belly red as she tiptoes
across the awning of our ribcage
maybe she meant you
maybe she meant us
& we didn't notice
love moving
from apple orchard
to tomato field to city just as the ghosts
in the abandoned hotel
roaming the hallways
room to room

> *our solar system migrating*
> *through galaxy migrating milky way*
> *through universe migrating*
> *through la boca de algún diosxx*

eternal the flower
the metaphor
the verb
the quetzal
y las colibrís

*

the long poem is nothing
but the weeping of a prayer
repeated through the beads
of a rosario
& a chirp

how is prayer not poem?
how is poem not prayer?
& we didn't see
how we smelled of america
our hands clasped over our mouths
quiéreme mucho

all of america
these whole bodies
are you
they are your breasts
your round hips
the soft skin folds of your waist
your stretched marked belly
your sex   *tu útero doloroso*
the warm in your armpits
the small of your back
the curls of your pubic hair
at the edges of your sex
the water coming off your limbs
the light smell of musk
                    miel quemada

after being en la pisca
piscando durazno
bombitas de sudor
en tu rostro
rotating getting lost
inside the hum of my body
                    this body that is yours
lost amongst a solar system of planets
rotating around their star
what poem is this?

19

if not a love poem
like the rest of goddxx's verbs
that were soccer balls y lágrimas
                              hurt uterus
behind an old high school's
track & field in an old farm town
that looks like corn fields in Missouri
but the soccer balls & the farm town
are in California

& the track & field has freshly mowed lawn
& the air is thick with freshly mowed lawn
& the locker room smells of an old leather baseball glove
from 3 generations past some stranger's heirloom
2 dollars at la segunda & you were happy
to finally have a baseball glove
you a mexican brown girl in the land of rushes
where the Patwin said
                    no, we burnt ourselves
                    so the chains can waffle
                    we begin life
                    you didn't colonize us
                    you didn't stand a chance
                    Tonantzin wearing the quetzal mask
                    carries us inside her armpit
acércate/mírame/mira el fuego
el clavo va naciendo
tu sombra detrás los cinco sentidos
¡grita! ¡tócame! ¡ámame!

en un abismo our heart stretches

to unknown capacities

like a memory becoming life again

*

remember how love walks on two feet?
                              remueve las horas
to the locker room puts on shorts a sports bra & a t-shirt
with holes in the armpits with armpit sweat stains
then runs kicks the soccer ball the grass damp
                              dampened earth
what a memory
americana youth
ag town
the quetzal body
inside our mouths
the quetzal's
feathery tail in our throat
the nopal on our foreheads
what were we doing?
                              surviving making el mundo dar vueltas
with the sky on our shoulders
we surrendered to summer breaks
gathering walnuts from walnut orchards
here there is un amorcito corazón estrellado
gazing at the creek gazing
at the tired lapping of a creek
named Putah Creek
an old creek that wasn't a puta
until we came along

& were you able to smell
the lavender growing that spring
that rare spring where every flower

bloomed alongside Putah Creek
       fireflies haciendo el amor

*

this is an erotic poem
that names hxrself
after a legion of nameless
angels

they were all here
on the grass of a track & field
the only track & field
of two towns over
where the summers
are full of gathering
almonds & corn,
sometimes tomatoes
& the angels
were like a fleet of
California gulls
sitting at the beach
huddled

what names
can I give you?

there was no siege
just me falling in love

how cruel

the gulls were also falling into love fluffy breasts
like everything that fell from that god in shining armor
like that feeling when you are playing
catch with no rules your sweaty fingers inside the leather glove
what a good feeling as the lights around the field come on
it is night time   la luna plateada

tus cachetes plateados
por fin tu enamorada y tierna

the cicadas horny
& you are alone digging
your cleats into the dirt
after a series of sprints

*

the dream is always
bursting
into something else

I am
spitting
word after word

can we tell
how the apple
falling from the
tree resembles
a recurrence of verb

america

I am reclaiming you

stealing back la semilla del frijol
el nopal my shield

in verb like that night
we first watched e.t
then went outside
tumbled at that age

the age of childhood

wonder & seeking climbing the alfalfa cubes
that were touching the night sky
as if they were giant city buildings
& within the gleam from stars
we got to the top our feet dangling
& then it rained the air steamy
the thunder popping
we were in the state of Idaho
somewhere near Boise

those days were something else
none of us spoke
English & barely did we know
what we were getting into

> *we fell in love*
> *cayéndonos entre nos*
> *como el primer cherubim*
> *estrellándose en nosotrxs*

we are americana
our brown
our quetzal
our colibrí chirp
on the yellow tractor
with its broken leather seat
with our amá driving
all of us gorgeous
with dirt rubbings on our foreheads
& on the fats of our bellies
niñez gorda en recuerdos
de almond orchards
tomato fields
& the sweet
treat of sweet corn
every so often
bathing our chubby bodies
at the levee
the sunset
gleaming

*

how do you explain this?
the chains we will soon turn
into powdery thick feathers
enveloping un cuerpo
in the same way
sand sinks

> *imagine the fluffing*
> *of a duckling*
> *the amount of care*
> *to make a glass rock*

how long will it take?
to see
the mirage of chains waffle
into wafting wings
there is no other way
to break it other than through the lips
of a lover & the body of a seraphim
who has the same amount of faith in language
a language that will finally transcend
but hasn't it transcended?

> *this tongue leaving us behind somewhere*
> *like the leftovers of a last supper & my apa getting high*
> *huffing glue somewhere in the tomato fields*
> *like it was the end of the world*

the moon is pulling at earth
the river swelling my lips growing heavy
cells speaking to make your heart
la lengua que tiene toda su fe en el Norte

> *things will be better en el Norte*

in the same way the monarchs' bodies
believe en el Norte

no thought to it just follow the sounds
of your body
as generations of bodies
come from the southern most part
landing here sometime in the spring
O imagine!
love!
O do love!
there is no other desire
but that dream
that hum
in our bodies
sex boca
sweat & tears

> *the definition of verb*
> *is you*
> *is us*

let us
clap our bodies
together
flood our
heart

*

the long poem remembers
seeing everything in fragments

not letting let me forget
about lung & my fragmented mind
there was never a fourth wall
to break

we were just a poem speaking
about itself

I am placing so much hope
on our insides our poemario

is this enough? our tripas gruñendo
we are carving each other
the song is growing enormous

a different city
is now being cut
into parts
parts that look like
your body
& my body
river & sea
the city is trying to be
our cheeks made into lakes
there is nothing
I could tell you that the stars
haven't mentioned nor the scars
that you carry

stars & scars
mirage the same
in the middle

of a softball game
just as tough
as flowers

wilting bowing amor to the reddening
silhouette of la virgencita
¿cuántas veces nos mataron?

aquí bailamos con los pétalos
el viento un suspiro de humo

*

I sat under constellations
& there you were

pétalos tiernos
peach fuzz shadows

un ser
aprendiendo
cómo ser un cherubim
allí con tu dolor
tragaste agua ardiente
te perdiste
entre las palabras
y suspiros de una loba
aun tus lágrimas calentitas
me dijiste

dame pan
para que no me
coman vivo
los espíritus

eres un milagro
how will the spirits eat you?
if not through a false metaphor
pero this is not a false metaphor
this is the howl of an old woman
descending mountain
an old mountain that is a goddxx
naming themselves with an x
she is howling
& so are the wolves
& the wolves her tribe
& on her shoulders hummingbirds swimming
the howl of the old woman

is the goddxx incarnate
trying to reach the angel's ribs & lungs
& she is the earth incarnate

leaping

with the tribe
her limbs long
un disparo de tu sudor
y nuestro sueño
¿qué somos?

si no muerte

ojo y calor
a stampede
of antelopes
wild horses
wolves mother wolves
licking each other
deer & unicorns
& every other body
leaping off the cliff

immortal los cielitos

¡mi vida!
somos sangre
caliente latiendo
suspiro caliente
iluminando
el sudor nos protege
sudor de loba
gritando
a la luna

*

& I could see
the syllables
of our bodies
become the embers
of firewood burning out

soft cold night

in the middle of pine
cedar woods
& I don't recall our campsite
but there you were
there I was
your mouth
holding a story
older than the makeup
around your eyes
the stars on your cheeks
reflecting firewood light
& like all the poets
I wanted to give this poem to you

raw

but I realized

raw is relative

it could mean medium rare to some
well done to others
& so I decided the most raw
would be if you pulled
the poem out from my chest
still breathing
then the poem
as it is pulled out
will have fog breath

outside este cuerpo steamy
will be warm for many full minutes
even in my palm it will be warm
as I pass it on warm and raw
still beating
because it still thinks it is alive
in the same way we offered sacrifices
when we believed
in the goddxxs
that made us

no nos mataron
somos el siempre
somos el nunca
noche lápiz lazuli
nuestra diosxx color querer
color fortaleza color tambor
vida morada como lo oscuro
de los cosmos
la cosa que nos da vida
nuestra Tonantzin con la máscara de la virgencita
el nopal en nuestra frente

& the goddxxs
that made you
& I were as young
as you & I
& then some

how things change
right?

suddenly your love craves
blueberry pancakes

& she is sweaty
so she makes the pancakes
for you & hot dang
you two smoke a joint
she lights incense
everything smells good
she smells great

                    blueberry tongue

just getting home
after some work
as a camera woman
hot dang
hot damn
it is all so gay

*

*San Francisco
is Bay Area cuerpos
all hip hop cumbia
mexican polka
& drum puro love
with some white fools
burning a man*

here we are
exotic
magic woman
making your shaman dream
come true
hah!
we don't give a fuck
we just changing
the newborn's baby diaper
in the same exact ways of
Maria Sabina
drinking a coke
or some aguardiente
con un cigarillo
our wrinkled lips
blowing you out
canción y duende

*

*

this poem writes hxrself
on a nightly moon   *swollen útero growing enormous*
                           hablándose como el agua

where you glance at me
& I glance
back at you
your thoughts under your skin
my thoughts under my skin
thought/less bombitas
easy verbs we blink together
like marbles on dirt
dirt on the corner
of a corn field
baby thumbs
thumbing them
during the hour
of high sun

                           the most dangerous
                           the light is
                           on our piel

said my abuelita
& so on
because we are exodus
making echoes
making future echoes
making past echoes
& so on
we go on
kissing fucking orgasm

if you will
is this a horny poem?
not at all
yes & everything
in between like the stink
in your crevices
especially your belly button
after a long day's work or sleep
whomever comes first is you
                    aquí besitos on your cutis

*

I am marimacha
making catholic mexican womxn
feel good in secret corners
feeling safe & grabbing my ass in lonesome city alleyways or
where the tomato fields curve high enough
to hide our immortality

esos files tristes como yo
eso files que nos comen vivas

I am that woMAN who's cuerpo
is like your mother's
stretch marks & soft panzacita
dark soft pubic hair
manos calientes
making love to you
on your darkest days
holding you nurturing
like your madre
I am that pocha
you glance at in the middle of misa
we both blushing about last night
I am that chicana toda jota
ESA LESBIANA
that makes your mouth water
NEPANTLA
to grab my nalgas
means your truth
& I am here for you
yes, you & I
joteando amando

al fin de todo tocando
nuestros labios

*

                    en esos tiempos comíamos diosxxs

la casa calentita con frijoles de la olla
mi abuelita Chona
tender with her tulips
& rose bushes
cupping my chubby cheeks
within her palms gruesos with the entire callo
del azadón the heat of a day entire on her face
the days of la pisca pesados on her shoulders
me decía

                              somos
                              marimachas
                              bien hechas

aquí estamos   *hermosas y*
                              fuertes como las flores de la barranca
a veces curanderas
a veces angelitas de la guardia
a veces Tonantzin
a veces Coatlicue
somos la noche la mañana la muerte despertando
                          heart ache entero atentas a la canción de todas
shimmering como las mariposas
que van entre pístale y pístele
flor entre flor huerta entre huerta
pero mas que todo las amantes
que curan tu corazón

*

my heart was broken
made into pieces
so we could finally see
each other

like Shakespeare's Romeo & Juliet
we were right there
under the blossom
of a walnut tree
& I saw

you were exodus
with the wings
of an archangel
& there we were
looking at each other
without saying nothing

the stars twinkled
I fell for you
maybe you did too

it wasn't easy
being quietly lesbian for you
I would have done it for a lifetime

that day your face
on my cuello
I just turned 13

you more of a woman

than I
at 17 years old
plump lips
wide hips

O you were beautiful
you are beautiful
in my youth/full
fantasy illusion

leaning into my left breast
O how my heart palpitated

resting your head under my chin
your cheeks warm on my neck

O how I fluttered

your deep lake brown eyes
looking at me your lips whispering
                    I love your flannel shirt
                    your smell
the next day
fuimos a un baile
in the middle of farm town
& there we were

you in the arms
of my primo
me at the doorway
of the dance floor

sweating like the marimacha
that I am

O americana

never hurt so bad
as you slipped your tongue
into my primo's mouth
the walnut orchards ripe
the moon una uña
my face salted lagrimas
the breeze through my armpits
a relief

*

as the bugs
with light on their butts
swam around the streetlamp
yellowing the street
into a warm yellow glow
we told each other this:

> *love is lust tus lágrimas en mi piel*
> *cuerpos aplaudiendo*
> *sudando so we can go on*
> *love is your lips sinking into the fat of my belly*
> *love is the part of your wings*
> *where their bone begins*
> *& love is our bones*
> *becoming a full moon*
> *banana leaf tamal*
> *after taste in my mouth & skin*
> *love is a whole pot of frijoles*
> *warm & ready for you & I*
> *love is maíz*
> *love is noticing the wrinkling*
> *of your hands*
> *how charming the wrinkles look*
> *on the curving of your cutis*

amor dormido   grítame
yo te estoy llorando
flor del nopal
toda rosa gruesa y dulce
mi boca llena de semillas
semillas en mis muelas mi lengua hinchada
así como nuestro seno lleno y piel gorda

piel que tú quieres
chupar

*

¿cómo me
mantienes ?
mar y tierra

                la mar
                lamando

¿cuál fondo?

                no hay fondo

me encabrono
toda encabronada
soy you
la luna es hermosa
mil voces mil bocas sangrando
tienes el mismo rostro de algún mundo cambiando
rodando

                lengua
                rodando

boca comiendo montaña y barranca
todo cambiando
todo, amor

*

I am a living womxn
daughter of Teocintle
daughter of Lourdes
daughter of Sofía
hueco of la Chonita
lucero de amor
hija with petals opening   *wilting/ no nos hincamos*
aquí estoy luna color hueso
toda cuerpo y carne
I hear the hoarse voice of you   *aguas*
                                   the layers of vulva

the mountain
the lake
the river
the sea
tectonic plates splitting
the aroma of your perfume odors
coming in as the day breaks
then again in the evening

tortilla quemada
comal on the fire

a remembrance
of all the womxn in my life
todas las palomitas y el último códex
pero no olvides la luna y su sol
todos los mundos entre nos
a song we made together
torso

mouth
cheek
hips
shoulders
muslos
mundos enteros
nothing no longer mine

        & I remember thinking my mind
        grew a lung like a nopal grows her flor
        as we got onto some train
        that would be faster than ever
        through the tunnel very vivid rock

aquí
el pan de cada día
eres tú
escarbando
tú

I go out
to every piece
of you beloved,
you are my war
my love entire
I am your soldier
I am your disciple
my uniform is the desert
& the great river
that leads
to the mouth of
your mouth
& I am on that great
river of yours
riding the current
looking for a place to fish
the water slapping my boat
& as I look for you
my lungs are bursting
saying I am a fisherwomxn
& soldadera for the word
of the word
of the song
for the song
that is inside the desert
& the mirage of
the pond of your
cuerpo
*

a fleet of angels
gathered gossiped
laughed cried
& ate fried fish
with nopales jitomate
y tortillas de maíz
using their hands
they indulged
their tongues

on this globo azul
their bellies full
they sleepy took a nap
on top of skyscrapers
& abandoned buildings
the bay area cityscape
grey colored with blue skies
some climbed into empty beds
or beds with a human sleeping
but they took a nap
with their bellies plump
& it seemed that a star lit sky began to arise

after a while they awoke confused
thinking they had been sleeping through a night
but the afternoon sun shone on their faces
awake they stretched their limbs
like the yawn of a dog or a wolf
they've never had so much time on their wings
it felt like goddxx was on vacation
anything was possible

anything is possible

& so they flew
the whole fleet
swimming in the air
in & around the cityscape
spray painting murals
here & there
tagging the bridges
getting high with the lonesome
& not so lonesome
they went about
hedonism all joy celebration
& when it came time to weep
they wept their tears with all of us
a cascade of love
as they sat on the peek of hills &
apartment buildings

the city lights
flickering
like two bodies
humping

*

I am your worst nightmare
with árabe eyes
marimacha heart
indio throat y labios
my whole body shaped
jota & tender
I am all throbbing
pigeon wide chest
corazón
tough como la flor
del nopal
I am stealing the sugar
cotton &
infinity.

SLUMBER

for a while, whether drunk
or sober at 2am i've been meaning to tell you to sleep
nursing on your belly
                    i slur
listen/ how puckered lips /sucking on plums
meaningless poet wanting to live
inside that/ sound of the angels' wings
and though you can hear them
just as the mumbling of brown speckled doves arriving on a window sill
after a long batch of rain
your eyes kept slurring
we kept disturbing
the wings outside our window
nothing made sense
as you opened your thighs cradled my head
the angels mimicked each other
still sucking on plums
we split the children in half
never/mind their little bodies
the river was strong enough
to swallow a desert whole
so it was easier for us to forget
the massive grave
an absolute miracle as we began
to squeeze our eyes shut
the wind picked up, knocking over
the empty garbage cans in the migrant camp
restless soul

the poet is becoming bitter
learning to dig for gold
and we wanted to sleep,
hoping the children would come home
i told you

i'll tell you a story

instead, you took my mouth wrapped it around
walls, all the while the angels were still there
and they began to whimper

the poet is dead the poet is dead

and we looked outside and inside
the walls splattered in red
limbs on our floor, small hands on our pillow
i've been wanting to tell you to go to sleep
with our knees covered in blood
never mind the rising sun
and the gust of wind

LA MARIPOSA Y SUS DUENDES

towards
a new direction
the monarch went
trying to avoid the nearness
of the sun

it took them over 300,000
generations,
before & not after

the beginning was essential
for the end

arriving on the day
of the dead

no one mentioned
how cloudy the skies seemed
the gravestones wiped clean
it was terrifying even
the phantoms couldn't find
their way

& we heard the awful sound
the ask for deliverance
by the riverbed

brown living waters
clasped against the desert
300,000

graceful wings drowned

the journey remarkable
it took both populations
several generations of bodies
to make a 6 to 9 month trek .

from north to south
for the winter
after the mothers dying
joining milkweed on the way back

alongside March
life begins again

eating leaf after leaf
they grow up
ready to fly without
knowing their mothers

they know
where to go

spreading pollen
the 2nd population
landing closer
to the sun

bronzing their bodies

by the time
we arrived it looked like the land
had swallowed the bodies
in secret we hoped for the bones
to surface

none of this would ever make sense
300, 000 of them rubbed to dust
we thought careless

eventually the prophet
goes blind naming two dreams
she couldn't bear a peoples' name
a prophet never could
see which population was
crossing the river
& name which one was
laying the children
it is easier to understand
the currents of the ocean

homeland
the Tigris river
transforms
on this side
half of the Euphrates'
sand tastes almost
the same as this body
submerging the land

today the moon is shaped
in our thumbs

waking mouths
pray to angels

heaven is becoming
robust tilled soil
madre tierra
we keep watering it
with blood
children of Abraham & Sarah

homeland
El Rio grande
O madre la tierra se muere
pero me dices
que nos va morder

hay pedazos de dientes
entre los files de tomate

y en la huerta de almendra
las mariposas se están
acabando

el río se está secando
y ya podemos ver los huesitos
de los nenes y nosotras hijas de Malinche

aún I was hoping

for the poem
to lead me
at least a waltz
that mirrored
our migrations

to answer something
about the unknown
breaking the fourth wall or the veil

between you and I
knowing that you
adore me

no need to say it
to each other

you are miraculously
made into three
sagrada trinidad
as I run my fingers
through your hair
the smell of your body on my body
& I know that you love me
in the same way a hummingbird
loves her flor generation upon generation
cuerpecitos entrándose
in the same way the leftover bones of the butterflies
are loved by the vast land
we are disappearing into

all of us together
forever

cariño,
I remember the first time
I held you in my arms
do you?

we were so new
& so soft

we took the N-Judah
to ocean beach
then you brought me to
the Tenderloin for some
good Thai food

I couldn't stop kissing you
on muni bus # 27 on the way
to your apartment on York St
in San Francisco

I learned to ride the bus
because of you
I fell in love with walking in this city
up hills & down hills
& I got a job here
serendipity
you taught me how to arrive

& we survived

making a home here

but do you remember?

how we forgot each other

how easily we got used to
jumping over torsos
strung out
passed out
limbs bleeding from
too many needle holes
even the woman covered in days old suet
& her period blood on her crotch
all crispy on her clothes
her eyelashes shimmering like ours
silencing a world around us
how we continued to get groceries
& read the news
all at once

bless the love
that continues
to love because I thought
we were all sober

it is impossible
not to say blood is
on our hands

life feeds on life
but I told you I have a story

>*a womxn dreams that she is a butterfly*
>*she awakes as a womxn, not knowing*
>*if she is a womxn or, if she is a monarch*
>*dreaming that she is a womxn*

who dreamt this? if not Borges' tiger
or Merwin's bear

what are we if not clay?

hurry up now
we are dreaming
the maker is talking
like the dead

only neither have a tongue
and I am lost in your
rainbow resembling
the long stretch of the river

aún el desierto
nos olvida
entre la crema de su polvo
y sus piernas secas
estamos aquí
deshaciendo el hacedor
haciendo la hacedora

no es un sueño
besar un colibrí
es un milagro

tu y yo
en lo azul de este mundo
hermosura
somos sin saber

I'll tell you though
to look out

the neighbors are saying
Abrahams' y Malichin's children
are killing each other
a hole through a railway

we all thought we could escape
it is true there are murderers
as we travel through
the tunnel

This poem that names hxrself Vuelta, erotic, slumber, y La mariposa is dedicated to the queer en el azadón, to the stink after a day piscando, to todas las mujxres en los campos trabajando, las que se llevaron en el femmecide--el femmecide que sigue comiendo nuestra tierra, the entire migration of each other, y siempre to my abuelita Chona that loved us no matter what, always a pot of frijoles for us.

"¡Arribia la Chona!"
bravo la Chona
y la Chona se mueve y la gente le grita

"...y todas las conocen con el apodo de Chona"
Mario Quintero de Los Tucanes de Tijuana

READING GUIDE

The poetics of place, the development of your tongue, & the culmination of your body entire that which is love.

Vuelta blends myth, and language to conjure the culmination of love & survival: love being the poet's body, the community & the hxstory it took for their body to arrive. The poet braids the inner voice to the outer voice & vice versa using the fragility of flower as metaphor for the delicate, miraculous existence of the brown queer migrant body. In the lineage of Gloria Anzualda, the poet reclaims their tongue & the atrocities that it took for their body to be here today. The poet's tongue reclaims, and refuses translation, allowing for translation to live within the movement of the poem, remaking myth, & using the act of epic poem as epistolary song. All of this is transcendence that recognizes that migration is an act of love & our tongues are a culmination of atrocity & migration: a wound that is healing revolts as it transforms & re-grows.

We all speak a migrating language.

Dear reader,

Our interaction with the movement of earth is connected to our tongue which is connected to our heritage which is connected to our politics, our place in the world, our view of the world finally to our truth, as a whole, as human beings. Every part of you is a miracle in itself—you peer into the world & the amount of time it has taken.

Thank you for reading below please find a series of prompts from the themes that live in the poems of Vuelta that will give you the release to celebrate your tongue and generate your poems. These prompts are a mixture of what has helped me articulate my poetics resulting from the work of Gloria Anzaldua, June Jordan's Poetry for the People, the oral song of my familia, & the poetry workshops that have opened up the essence of poem for me. Importantly, I ask you to recognize the voices that came before you to allow for the word that you form now. Our voices & our poem does not arrive in a vacuum.

THEME: THE POETICS OF PLACE

WRITING WARM-UP: Make a list of sensory details of your own neighborhood. Write down at least ten things that come to your mind. What does your neighborhood sound like at 9 pm? Who is on your block on a Saturday afternoon? What does your kitchen smell like? If your back was to your front door and you looked left to right out in the street, what would they see? If I lived across town from you what are the places I would need to walk through to get to your casa? What are the nicknames of people in the neighborhood? Who's in the living room? What do people do for work?

PROMPT:

Tell about a place that you are from. Use imagery, sensory, & your intimate voice to tell me about a place that you are from. Can you see, feel, taste, hear, and smell where you are from? What are the colors of your sunset? Your sunrise? What is the evening sound, feel, and smell like? Who is with you? What song is playing? Are you singing? (Allow yourself to break into song)

THEME: LOVE

Love is often defined through a romantic binary lens. In this exercise, I ask you to shift that lens to the acts that allow for gratitude of our existence. Take a moment to recognize your body and how long it has carried you. Love exists in different forms & movements, love can be noticing the wrinkling on someone dear to you, planting seeds, cooking a meal, the way your hands move like your mother's or your sister's, or the way you bring food to your mouth is just like how your abuelito did, or the way you let a laugh slip from your mouth.

PROMPT:

1. Pick a verse, a stanza from this collection or another collection, or a song you adore & launch your own poem– beginning or ending with that line or stanza.

2. Write an anthem, a song, a poem, that speaks to this moment, that speaks to you, speaks to your community, that will energize you, your readers, and your community. Think about the power of repetition. Think about the communities you inhabit & your love for them.

THEME: YOUR TONGUE/VOICE/ LANGUAGE

Your voice is unique to you, with it you bring your entire life experiences. Essentially your voice is how you have learned to use the tool called language. Your voice is you and only yours, it comes from the deepest part of you.

*Language evolves as scars do, language is a scar built upon another scar, think of your hxrstories. Do you hear your ancestors, your chosen ancestors? How do they speak to you?

Warm-up writing embracing your voice, and the intersections it moves through.

Think of your language, your private language, the words you use inside yourself, the words you use when you are exchanging among your communities, among your friends, family, lover, or lovers. Think of the poem as an extension of all this as you make your poem.

What is our language? What are the different ways we talk to each other? How do we communicate in different spaces that we walk through or encompass during the day? During our lives? What is the language of our ancestors? How does it exist in us today?

PROMPTS:

1. Write a letter to someone dear to you from the past or present using the speak you use with them

2. Write a letter or a poem or a song to a loved one, your abuelita, a chosen ancestor, and then write a letter in response with the languages they use with you.

3. Think of a special moment from your childhood that has stuck to your body, your memory—something that made you feel safe & good. Write this memory down to the best of your ability. Don't hold back or edit yourself—free write! Use your senses, memory of smell, sounds, sounds of words–everything that brings you comfort.

As you move through these prompts & generate your work of love, send it out into the world, share with your communities & loved ones. Gracias con todo mi corazxn. Here's to making our song enormous, here's to sharing in poem!

Un fuerte abrazo
Su,
Lourdes

ACKNOWLEDGMENTS

My song is indebted to all the mujxrs in my lineage. To us who continue to survive this tierra femmecide. To the tambor that has crossed continents to arrive and form the gut I carry today.

Like all of our work as hacedoras, this is a culmination of the bodies that came before me. None of this would have been possible if my abuelito had not passed on in the tomato fields of Yuba City in the late 1950's nor the pain my father inherited & passed on to me. I want to acknowledge the strife & endurance my ama, my siblings and I have pushed through in this country. We are who we are & we are beautiful. Blessed we are and a blessing we are to this world & this reality. Our brown body is miraculous. Pa Mi amá Lourdes Sofia Figueroa Medina–gracias por todo su sacrificio todo el amor que nos sigues dando. To my siblings Rosanna, Anuar, Carlitos, y Jose Emilio, mi tio Carlos, y mi primo Jorge Uriel Medina, you are an entire miracle blessing this earth. Aqui este librito de amor pa ustedes, amor completito, you are hacedores in your own right descendants of the nopal. Let us continue to heal & heal this world.

My deepest gratitude to Lupe Ortiz, who worked for the Migrant Education Program when I was in high school in the 1990'sl. Ella que trabajó for our gente de los campos de Yolo County, & somehow plucked me out in high school putting me on a path toward college, service & beyond. Lupe Ortiz taught me the ideals that I continue to work with today, that of service & love, that of making our own tables & breaking down doors that do not serve our people. Because of Lupe so many of us had the opportunity to move forward, she loved us all, migrant farmworker kids & gave us a safe space. Winters High was lucky to have her, she did more for our people than anybody ever did at the time, a true revolutionary, a true heart for la raza, with Lupe I learned the meaning of our pueblo–she passed on to the other side too soon.

Siempre to my abuelita Chona who continuously whispered in my ear that I am loved & I will be what I am no matter what. Head fast with muscled arms she moved forward and killed rattlesnakes in a blink of an eye.

I want to thank Kim Shuck & Doug Salin for embracing Peggy & me, collaborating & loving us, bringing us home literally & figuratively in the bay area. Kim, who continues to break down doors & make her own table larger & full of love, her unconditional support of my voice has propelled me to spaces that are genuine & revolución. Aqui este librito de amor pa ustedes.

As I continue to write about our lives in Yolo County, I am indebted to the Patwin nation, the people of the West Winds who refused colonization and burnt themselves to the other side. I dreamt you in my 11-year-old body without knowing you, the night we first arrived at Yolo Housing. Looking out to the land I saw patches of fire, humo, blue skies, naked trees, bearded white men in blue & you in your huts piles of fire burning around me. Let these words continue your prophecy of love y revolución.

Aqui la palabra es the lineage of Malichin, Sor Juana Inez de la Cruz, Gloria Anzaldua, June Jordan, Rosario Castellanos, y los cuentos de mi abuelita Chona.

This librito is for presses like Nomadic Press, for the community you continue to build, for making your own table out of love, you are a true revolución, the medicine that is giving all of us the next world– gracias J.K. Fowler, MK Chavez, & Laura Salazar for believing in this song.

I want to thank Norma Cole, a continuous mentor & poet teacher, who embraced me from the first moment we met. Introducing me to the poem outside the americas, to loving me as love entire–because of you, I learned where pieces of my tongue came from. Our friendship over the years as we meet randomly for coffee or tea continues to grow & fill me–we are meant to be, I too am grateful we have each other.

I am indebted to my poetry writing group & continuous love: Karen Llagas, Florencia Milito, Tehmina Khan, Abigail Licad, Shradha Shah, & Mark Prudwosky here this librito for you.

I am indebted to Edwin Lozada one of the first to support, mentor & love me here in San Francisco, a poet hero & artist that embraces the Spanish tongue & the tongue beyond.

For Pio Candelario you left me too soon with drafts of poems & plays & dreams about our people–the migrant farmworkers. I miss you & our meals together at 55 Polk Street when you came over with papeles in hand, my poems made into your plays, & how you giggled, especially that night I dropped you off at your painting class & you said as you hopped out the car into the night "I came to San Francisco to be an artist! HA HA!" thank you for taking Angelica and me out when we were burnt out from the politics of San Francisco City Hall & the immense pain resulting from this damn schism, duende, duende you are.

For Carla Valdez, Kevin Killian & Dodie Bellamy, Paolo Peralta, Sarah Gaugler, Michael & Pat Gaugler, Wilfred Galila, Hassan Said, Jamie Townsend, J. Worthen, Cinthia Marisol Lozano, Judy Garcia, Baruch Porras, Suzanne Gladney, Angelica Cabande, Lian Ladia, Samantha Tieu, Margaret Guzman (de buena familia), Aisha

Ahmad, Michelle Marie Robles Wallace, Lily Chien-Davis, Josiah Luis Alderete, Angel Dominguez, Aaron Shurin, Brian Teare, Steve Dickinson, Tatiana Luboviski-Acosta, E.K Keith, Thea Matthews, Eric Garcia & Kat Cole (detour dance), the Paru-paru y Colibrí Workshop Poets & always Prof Alena A. Hairston for changing the trajectory of my work forever putting me in the path of poem, este librito for you all.

Aquí le doy las gracias total a mi editor MK Chavez a poet genius, a true caretaker of voz y amor. Gracias for your heart full embrace, here Pachamama for the word, illumination out of love– the work could not have transcended to this place without you, my admiration & love for you

To my forever collaborator y lover Peggy Peralta, thank you for your patience, your unconditional support, your buddhaness, your rice belly, intense love for the ocean, & books–this life of poetry would & could not have been possible without you, here's to our hustle of love

Siempre to Gloria Anzualda y la Maria Sabina for the verb & verbation of each other. To all of us, mestizaje– brown & black—colonization & all the terrifying atrocities that did not destroy us. We are still here conscious & full of canción—keep making the song enormous, the cosmos all around us, love is all around us and in us.

Thank you to elderly, Mirage, & Night Music Journal for publishing earlier versions & pieces of Vuelta

Gracias a todos por su amor entero

LOURDES FIGUEROA

Lourdes Figueroa is an oral poet. Her poems are a dialogue of her lived experience when her family worked in el azadón in Yolo County. The words el azadón are used by the ones who work in the fields—the work of tilling the soil under the blistering sun. She is the author of the chapbooks *yolotl* and *Ruidos = To Learn Speak*, completed during her Alley Cat Books Residency. She received her MFA in Poetry at the University of San Francisco. She is a recipient of the 2021 Nomadic Press Literary Award in Poetry selected by emeritus poet Laureate Kim Shuck. She works and lives in Oakland with her wife, filmmaker, Peggy Peralta. Together in July of 2020 they launched Bilbil Projects, a space where poem & film come together. Lourdes is a native of limbo nation. Lourdes continues to believe in your lung and your throat.

4 OTHER WAYS TO
SUPPORT NOMADIC PRESS WRITERS

Please consider supporting these funds. You can donate on a one-time or monthly basis from $10–∞ You can also more generally support Nomadic Press by donating to our general fund via nomadicpress.org/donate and by continuing to buy our books.

As always, thank you for your support!

Scan the QR code for more information and/or to donate.

You can also donate at nomadicpress.org/store.

ABOUT THE FUNDS

XALAPA
FUND

XALAPA FUND

The Xalapa Fund was started in May of 2022 to help offset the airfare costs of Nomadic Press authors to travel to our new retreat space in Xalapa, Veracruz in Mexico. Funds of up to $350 will be dispersed to any Nomadic Press published author who wishes to travel to Xalapa. The funds are kept in a separate bank account and disbursements are overseen by three (3) Nomadic Press authors and Founding Publisher J. K. Fowler.

Inherent in these movements will be cultural exchanges and Nomadic Press will launch a reading series based out of the bookstore/cafe downstairs from the space in August 2022. This series will feature Xalapa-based writers and musicians as well as open-mic slots and will be live streamed to build out relationships between our communities in Oakland, California, Philadelphia, Pennsylvania, and the greater US (and beyond).